Best wi~

[signature]

13.11.99

THOUGHTFUL SOLITUDE

Alison Edwards

MINERVA PRESS

LONDON

MONTREUX   WASHINGTON   SYDNEY

THOUGHTFUL SOLITUDE
Copyright © Alison Edwards 1998

All Rights Reserved

ISBN 1 86106 252 4

First Published 1998 by
MINERVA PRESS
195 Knightbridge
London SW7 1RE

Printed in Great Britain for Minerva Press

THOUGHTFUL SOLITUDE

To my parents

Contents

Germination

Vernality

Philosophy I (Body)

Philosophy II (Mind)

Mortality

Germination

Entry

Like some subterranean storm
You entered this passage –
The passage which gives and receives life.
A cliché it was not.
Unique it was.
It was no invasion
But a carefully planned
Reconciliation;
A tender treaty,
A subversive signal.
You were the master:
Mellifluous,
Melancholy, moody,
Searching for my entry
Barred from many.
Not a traitor, but as a
Conspirator you
Discovered my womanly weakness
Under the guise of master.
Manifold mirages
Come. And go.
You come and go,
A spirit perhaps,
Traversing no man's land, but yours.

His Touch

His touch
Tempted the tenuous
Tendrils, the tense
Tops, the tender
Tips.
Together
We two
Trembled, and terrorised
The touch.

First Time Love

It's the first day scent
On a first day cover.
It's the breathtaking freshness
Of a new babe and mother.

It's the skin-splitting crunch
Of a Golden Delicious.
It's the hopes and desires
Of dreams not fictitious.

It's the deep, earthy smell
Of a new leather bag.
It's that last special draw
On the very first fag.

It's the waft of the surf
On a warm summer day.
It's the homecoming aroma
Of fresh, gathered hay.

It's the old garden fire
Embracing the air –
It's that glorious feeling
Of your first love affair.

Love

Here
It comes
Swallowing, scintillating, seductive,
Surreptitiously leading all suitors away
On its voluptuous virgin curve.
Serenely white
Yet
Demonically daring
Us
Towards
Fulfilment.

Love's Lost

As I left I was
Prepared for tears.
Oh yes!
Over the times we shared.
The mesmeric moments
Were gone, I thought.
And our last words were
'Probationary', preparing me
For the fact that I would NEVER
Feel your touch again.

There were empty days
And nights for me alone, when
In dreams I would relive
The moments you were inside me,
Yet feel incomplete.

We are no longer together.

Love's Lost II

Sultry days
Of weeks gone by.
Time flies by.
Isolation comes and goes.
Is my home but an island?
Have I been cast away
By my own stupidity?
Rejection enslaves me.
The sun has disappeared,
It happened as I left.
Now miles away from him
I feel suddenly alone.
The cold unreceptivity
Of the moon is all I have.
An outcast of my own sensibilities.
As I lie here my thoughts go back
To a recent past.
My feet crumbled under a
Cloud of vermilion passion,
A blood red sky
Turned to grey despair.
As I left
Torture and torment left with me.
Who was and is spinning my web
Of life?
Incorrigible, unfathomable,
Answerless.

Parting of Ways

Motionless and speechless
I stood there.
Drained of everything.
Hope, once torrential in its intensity,
Had vanished.
Feelings, so genuine in their purity,
Had been abused.
Love, so real and tangible, or so I thought,
Had been cheapened
To a knock-down price.
Emotions had been steam-rollered.
My once strong, rounded personality
Was now as weak as cracked porcelain.
As I stood there
Heartbreak was on display,
A lonely figure, bag in hand –
Why was I the fool
And he the escapee?

Short-Sighted Thoughtfulness

You stupid hand and mind,
You short-sighted thoughtfulness,
Rushing headlong as always, like some
Languishing lemming suddenly struck
Lifefully by the vibrancy of existence
And the need to express again
Achievement.

You silly hand that imprisoned the pen,
You frivolous mind that linked the words,
Line after line – once innocent and pressure-free –
Bulged and blossomed into this rare feeling of
Exuberance.

You simplistic appendage of my arm,
You overflowing foolish mind.
There was no point in it.
It had no purpose.
What could you gain from it?

Put it down to youthful excitement
And it brings crow's feet to my eyeline.
Attribute it to impassioned pleadings
For recognition
And it gnaws at my self and its dignity.

There was no reason.
It was proven purposeless.

I gained nothing from this
Intentioned friendship gesture, save
The usual wave-strong, all too rock-infested
Feelings of
Anguish – for my short-sighted thoughtfulness,
Realisation – in my long-visioned stupidity,
And more rock-like in its pain than these
Two fellows,
Regret – for my oh, so stupid flowing hand
And my all too trusting mind.

Defenceless Emotions

The fear of loss of contact
Confounds me.
The despair of no news
Nags me.
The non-hearing of your voice
Vexes me.
The absence of your smile
Silences me.
The loneliness without your handshake
Haunts me.
The emptiness without your eyes
Envelops me.

And suddenly I feel –
Despair, Vexation, Haunting Silences,
Doubts, Fears.
All these and more
Enclose me as I realise
– THAT WAS IT –

Those brief cursory moments
When two hearts and minds
Fused and unfused,
Joined and severed,
Almost 'clicked' –
Then went their separate ways.

Never to feel the same again,
Never to be the same again,
But also and more poignantly,
Never to meet again.

These are the moments
That make
Life a bitch.

Vernality

Hope

Look!
Over there!
Can't you see it?
It *is* there!
Fine and sheer,
It may be.
Difficult to
Appreciate
From a distance, yes!
Look!
Sylph-like
Swoopings,
Amazing agility
Pushing forth
Through the
Air.
Gently caressing.
Look!
It could miss you!
Colourless,
Tasteless,
But look!
Over there!
It's coming closer!
Go to meet it!
Don't begrudge
The long journey

It has had.
It's here!
Now!
Look – beside you!

Spring

I saw it today.
It was small,
Minute even –
Perhaps almost
Invisible.

If I had walked too fast
Or too recklessly
I might have missed
Or even destroyed it.

It was just peeking out
Of its homeliness –
Only enough to show
The smallest trace of
Colour.
A trace, yes –
But enough for me.

I saw it today
In all its fragile feminine glory,
Isolated yet amiable.
It delivered its message
Loud and clear.
"Spring is here!"
Resounded from
The delicate form
Of the crocus.

Spring's Sentinel

Everywhere
Its yellow hue looks
Delightful.

Its delicate form
Dominates
Everywhere.

Its subtle fragrance
Spreads
Ethereally.

Spring's sentinel
Lightens
Even the darkest inlet.

This is exquisite lightness –
Style personified,
Simplicity yet abundance –
All found in the
Feisty form of the daffodil.

It feels at ease in the wild meadow,
Producing copious carpets of colour,
It is at home in the Shelley vase
On the corner of the uplighting and uplifted mantel.

The daffodil is a stalwart breed,
The everlasting signal of
Life renewed.
Once it arrives, colour manifests itself
Everywhere.

Spring's Pregnancy

It has crept up on me again,
Again, I ask myself – is it worth the pain?
The pain within as I burst forth,
Forth into a world still sleeping,
Sleeping off the effects of winter's ice orgy.

Every year the pain returns to me,
To me! With a vengeance I cannot explain.

I too have enjoyed the ice months,
Months so cold on the surface yet –
Yet for me in subterranean satisfaction all was warm,
Warm throughout but...

Every year the pain returns to me,
To me! With a vengeance I cannot explain.

I have to be strong and endure 'it'.
'It' is the process of birth and rebirth –
Rebirth for me in my entirety, birth for the
New Spring.

I push through the earth forcefully,
Forcefully, yet careful not to destroy my delicate offspring,
Offspring that will delight and develop.

No epidural for me!
Every year the pain returns to me,
To me! With a vengeance I cannot explain,
And a joy I will always remember.

Philosophy I (Body)

The Man

Stretching ahead of me
I see frantic faces,
Money-filled purses
Food-filled bodies –
All racing and ignoring
The man.

He, like some Miltonesque caricature,
Stands shakily.
His face is frantic, too,
But frantic with disappointment.
He has no purse and no money,
His body is full of emptiness.
His heart races, he is ignored,
The man.

I always imagine
The man
To have lost his real self.
Surely he was happy once –
At least once,
Maybe only once!

His clothes are his trademark,
Like lacerated flesh
They gape – jaws open wide,
Desperately craving – what?

33

Unshaven and heavy with the scent of dirt
The man
Begs beautifully.

The rot-filled streets are his hideaway;
The mephitic rubbish bins,
Nasally congested with our supposed dross,
Become his food source.

I feel dispirited
By the man and
Stretching ahead of me
I see frantic faces,
Despair-filled purses,
Death-filled bodies,
All racing and today,
Ignoring each other.

Vocal Indiscretions

elonGated sentences fly uncontrollably away,
wOrds full of effervescence and life,
cordial intonations Skipping from lip to lip,
Sanctimonious females causing strife,
lapping up all indiscrIminate flaws
to be found in every Person's life.

all of uS succumb to

G O S S I P

Winning Feelings

From the murky pit of my stomach
It rose and welled up.
My cheeks felt fire-filled.
It was an icy penetrating warmth,
Not experienced in a long time.
It moved rapidly and precisely
To my hands.
They began to shake.
Me, trembling?
Never!
Onward on its dedicated course
It rushed,
Speedily affecting my near perfect pulse
And regular heartbeat.
Banging, I felt my heart bulge
Uncontrollably.
Me, uncontrollable?
Never!
Desirous palpitations, blushes, or that
'Glowing feeling' engulfed me.
Legs, normally tree-like in their solidity,
Visibly trembled.
Fear or love normally preside over these feelings.
Why did I feel so good?
You've guessed –
I won the Lottery last night!

The Eyebrow I

Two we have, each one perched
High and mighty above all other features,
Each reflecting, responding, reacting.

Elongated they may be
Yes, and small, or wide or bushy or dense.
Expressive they certainly are.
Beautifully fluid, they show
Rapidly our true reactions – but,
Only the few see them as they are:
Windows to our personalities.

Eyebrows II

Rising and falling,
Creased with happiness or sorrow,
Densely furrowed in thoughtful thoughts,
They mirror movements and moods magically
And guilelessly.
They can be devious,
Likewise seductive.
Plucked thinly or wildly left untamed
They arch and frame
Our every deed.

Temptation

It stands there in smug satisfaction,
Tempting me.

Its rounded or rotund form bulges,
Calling me.

It has a homely, cosy appearance,
Warming me.

It leans forward perilously,
Rousing me.

It encapsulates all positive features,
Luring me
To grasp its homely limb
And enable its gushing, warming
Self to rush to freedom.
It cascades forth,
And fills me with a smug
satisfaction,
In the form of a
Cup of tea.

False Teeth

False teeth are false teeth
Or so I thought –
Until a pair broke in front of me.

Paradise was not lost *à la* Milton
But masticatory freedom was.
Toothless familiar people
Look strange.
Somehow empty, the face leers
Pathetically.
It should be funny, but
I feel sad.
Without them, trusted faces change
Becoming helpless and droopy.

False teeth are not homeless.
They have their plush 'semi'
In a glass by the bed,
You remove them like curlers.
Replace them and
The wearer feels at home,
Life looks more rounded –
More upwardly mobile.

I don't want to be a toothless wonder,
I want my teeth to have a proper home,
Solid roots and all!
Get my toothpaste and my dentist's number
Now!

Patience

Patience is a tool, you know,
I do not handle well,
It requires a deal of stamina
And the power not to dwell
On all the things that might occur
And the things that never will,
So you see I've never mastered
The art of sitting still,
And waiting, not pre-empting
The moments still to come,
I'd rather greet the blackest side
Than sit patiently and hum.

I've never found it easy
To look for silver linings,
Instead I find it simpler
To castigate with whinings
The thoughts which always lead me on
To feel despair, not joy,
And meet each new day dawning
With bleak thoughts that do annoy
And irritate and worsen
My already furrowed brow –
Oh, I wish that I were patient –
Please God, just teach me *how.*

Sleep

Sleepful slumbers.
Sultry selections.
Cunning curses.
Dastardly devisings.
The unreal reality
Which protects us from
Ourselves.

Shadows

Flickering moments,
Extensive views
Of man – alone though
Not lonely.
The shadow
A personal possession –
Elusive always.
Is man the shadow?
Is the shadow an extra impregnable limb?

Bleakly fragile
Sultry silhouettes,
Seething seductively,
Desperately devising,
Deceptively daring,
Stretching in their own surrealism.

Up there, twirling,
A visible form
Of our ethereal selves.
Hyphens,
Helpless in their own unreceptivity.
We try to touch, to grasp them –
Our better selves. We fail.
Soluble, transparent, our spirit in life.
Shadows, like spirits,
Slip stealthily away
Leaving us alone.

Who Am I?

Threatened
Yet threatening –
Who am I?

Feared
Yet fearing –
Who am I?

Confused
Yet confusing –
Who am I?

Unloved,
Loved
And loving –
Who am I?

Duality yet singularity,
Parallelisms in my soul.

Life

Life is everywhere.
It is removed
Yet removing,
On occasions
Earth-shattering and
Cataclysmic.
It becomes us,
We become it.
Enveloping and enveloped
By this formless form,
This fruitless fruit,
This engenderer.
It gives but takes.
Similarly we take,
But do we give back
When we receive?
This created creation
Creates, develops and destroys.
It is the question begging
Question,
It is the answerless answer.
It is our enigma.

Philosophy II (Mind)

Curiosity

I am not obsessed.
I am just curious,
And eager to know.
That's why I'm restless,
Constantly moving.
That's why I'm lost,
Constantly searching.
"What for?" I ask myself.
Time and
Again the answer:
"Who knows?"
But I am not obsessed,
Just curious
To find the answers
To my questions,
The plusses
To my minuses,
The fullness
To my emptiness,
The friendship
To my loneliness.
But
I am not obsessed.

Tolstoy's Dilemma[1]

The incredible solitude of being was desired,
Splendid solitude in isolative conditions:
A no man's land – or woman's, it seemed.
The harping high-pitched contradictions,
Life devised, eroded the spirit
Once overburdened with thoughts and aims,
Now understressed with familial dissent.

Here was a large, answerful being, taunted
By emotional feelings of love, doubt, fear,
Emotions unique and intertwined, which
Fearlessly disrobe us all
And leave us – like him – dressed in
Despairing frustration.
His once silk-like fleshy theories now
Embodied for eternity in the rough,
Coarse trappings of a living corpse.

A pre-Brechtian complex form –
Fixated with the malaise of life.

Here was a great tortured idol, being idolised,
Canonised almost and feeling suffocated
By an ever demanding negative–positive:
An antithesis yes, but this positive–negative
Was, and is, life.

[1] Based on *Tolstoy*, a play written by James Goldman.

Without these contrasting forces
Pulling our and his life strings,
Life itself expires, withering willessly in
Self-imposed confinement.

Here was Tolstoy, all ideas to all intellectuals,
All inspiration to all people, a man, who –
Minus his negative, inbred Sonian wealth –
Overdosed on positive freedom,
And his splendid isolation became
An inverted resting place but...

There was no rest.
There could be no rest,
Just solitary despair, and the realisation that
Life needs a positive–negative balance.

Too late this was achieved.
For him – but not for us!

Disappointment

Disappointment

is

this –

It's the blank page on the book of life,
It's the constant battle with problems and strife,
It's the empty feelings at the end of the day,
It's those lonely hours when in bed you say:
"What *did* go wrong? Was I *so* bad?
How are *they* so happy and I feel *so* sad?"

It's the gnawing fear of chances all gone,
It's the chilling reminders in a favourite love song,
It's the clammy clenched fists filled with sheer despair,
It's the moment you shout, "Why is life so unfair?"

It's those missed opportunities knocking the door,
"Why do I have less hope and others have more?"
It's that moment in time – you feel lost and alone
And return to the foetal position at home.

Disappointment

is

this

and more...

"But what's that I hear knocking at my door?"

Schadenfreude

Guilty!
Yes. I am.
You are.
We all are.
Of
Schadenfreude.

That malicious moment when
'We've done' what 'the others'
Have not.
Glorious gloating pervades the air,
More fragile than finest silk.

Schadenfreude
Is silk-like in its ability to
Infiltrate the invisible cracks
In life, in minds, in thoughts.

Gleefully we thunderously applaud
Life's anti-goods,
Life's positive ills for them – not us.
Like rampageous predators,
We devour each succulent
Morsel of despair,
As fellow *Homo sapiens*
Run amok and stampede vaingloriously
Towards our – not their – success.

Instead of *Freude* gaining speed
It becomes tranquillised and crumbles,
Sheath after silken sheath,
Into stupor-like *Schade*.

Then
Guilt rears its melancholy head
As we realise our gleeful, euphoric delight,
In our neighbour's failure and our *Wunder*
Was
Falsch.

Conundrum

Somnambulistic signals.
Are they tormenting?
Tortuous?

Metaphoric messages.
Are they solid?
Stultifying?

Cacophonous cyclones.
Are they moving?
Melodious?

Gargolic greetings.
Are they
Proving
Peaceful?

Quidnunc

Quite
Unlike me
It was to
Delve.

Nonsensical!
Useless!
Never again!
Carrying
Sense aside.

Escape

Heads spin
Whirling, wily, wiry, wilting.
Is that you I see?
Gorgeously grotesque
On a high too?
"Too good," you say, "too truthful."
My escape is to this transitory world
Where the best things go – quickly.

This world will disappear on the
Wide horizon of tomorrow's reality.
But –
In a state of subconscious sublimity
My cares now disperse,
My dreams now increase,
Up that hill I race
And race and
As the summit spears itself before me
It is submersed by wakefulness
By a perverted, eternal truth.
Utopia vanished.

Let Time Dictate Your Rushes

Too much, too soon, too good –
Be patient.
Too much, too soon, too good –
Be still.
Too much, too soon, too good –
Be thoughtful,
And wait – on the edge,
Until things come – halfway.

To yearn, to desire too much
Is fallacy.
The fallacy of a man
Fallen.
Don't let this happen.
To yearn, to desire too soon
Is intolerance.
Intolerance of a life
Soon ruined.
To yearn, to desire too good
Is despair.
Despair with yourself.

See time as a friend
And you will achieve.
Yearn for something – much, but not too much.
Desire for something – soon, but not too soon.

Don't leave yourself too soon.
Don't pull away too much.
Don't think yourself too good.
Don't make time your master.

Time can and will misplace you and your dreams,
Leaving you with nothing but an empty vacuum.

Mortality

Phone Call

Come on!
Come ON!
Ring up!
Ring UP!
Ring, ring!
RING! RING!
Hallo!
Who's there?
Wrong Number –
DESPAIR!

Night Creeps Upon Me

Painful – throbbing – Night creeps upon me,
Like a shadow of demonic Death.
How do I escape its enveloping Self?
Is there a way out from this Land
That changes Daydreams into
Nightdreams?
I yearn for some Utopia, without this
Starless Selfless Existence.
Is Night the Escape?

Night and Sleep are the
Dragons we chase
To escape from Light.
We know that
Night
Is Death's Counterfeit Act.

My Brave One

Touch tenderly my hand,
My brave one.
Give me the strength I crave,
My brave one.
You are my steadfast hope,
My true one.
The pain I suffer,
I suffer as silently as I can,
You know
My brave one.

Hallucinations haunt me –
Why?
My past permeates my waking hours,
My brave one.
I witness again my turbulent youth.
Touch tenderly my hand.

My brave one,
You understand my fears.
I fear leaving –
Not leaving life,
But you,
My brave one, and
Your positive force
Of care
Throughout my life.

Touch tenderly my hand.
I have to go.
But I will always
Be near,
Touching you tenderly
As you touched me,
And helped me
With warmth
Down a long, lonely path.

Life's Last Journey

Suffering belched forth – the stench was nauseous,
Life took on the familiar feared transitory form.
The once sturdy body, visibly withered
Before my pain-stricken eyes.

I suffered, too, the mental anguish.

We were all on the rack,
Being stretched limb from limb,
Hope from hope.

Life was being wrenched horribly away.
Those strong safe hands,
Once as large and impenetrable as
Rock formations for me,
Had shrunk.
Bones, once heavily protected by invigorating
Bodily health, took on the guise of
Stalagmites – projecting purposefully,
And bravely
On the Calvary journey.

No Stations of The Cross here, but
Passionate feelings abounded in us all.
This Gethsemane was too close for comfort.
Was there no justice? No hope? No love?

Granite foundations, presumed to be
Unshakeable, were crumbling
In this stoic lonely battle.

The bodily form became life's alias.
Instead of concrete I saw glass,
Arrogantly awaiting its fragile end.
It was like touching a slice of chronic vulnerability.
So, I did not touch.

This was stoicism.
This was metamorphosis
From life and to life everlasting.

But the vision I shall always remember
Is painful anguish.

The Snowstorm

Sitting sullenly in isolation,
I look out on a virginal white landscape,
I know so well but cannot recognise.
Cars in front stretch onward,
Like densely packed miniature mobile homes.
We are all imprisoned by the snowstorm.

It came suddenly.
Suddenly, it halted everything.
Innocent and idyllic it may look,
But it has a deceptive quality
Which dupes us all.

For children snow is a creating force.
Models and images, ideals can be evolved
From this quicksilver natural force.
These models have no longevity.
And children weep when their 'masterpieces'
Disappear.

Snow is cruel.
For adults, snow is a reminder of a childhood lost,
Quick melted in time.
But more than this now, snow
Is a destructing force
Showing clearly the ruinous ruts of our lives.

Simultaneous love and hate of this substance
Fill us to overflowing.
Sitting sullenly in isolation
Gives adults thinking and fearing space –
Instead of evocative and hopeful *when*s
Our momentary fears instil *what ifs*.

Like caged animals we peer petrified through
The snow-infested landscape, and
Suddenly, from halting, we are moving –
Our minds jolt from passive fear to first gear thrust
And once again I think of 'when...'

Winter's Assault

Winter spreads itself out like some all encompassing mantle
Of inverted warmth.
There is no escape from its power.

Nature itself quivers in anxious anticipation.
"Here it comes!" the petals say
As they regally fall from angelic grace.
They form wizened shapes and lose
Their delicious beauty instantly.

Lustrous greens and vivid yellows disappear,
A sallow cancerous hue radiates from the landscape.
Abundance and unavoidable natural excesses
Have taken on the guise of
Barren bleakness.

Trees once manifestly gorgeous
With branches greenwashed with leaves
Have been ceremoniously stripped
By winter's rape-infested hands
And now stand nude.

There is no escape from its power.

Time

Tick! Tick! Tick! Tick!
Time marches onward
With the practised precision
Of a regimental body.
It doesn't stop –
Ever.
We fear time,
It goes too quickly,
It is a quickstep,
It is a downward spiralling force.
It doesn't stop –
Ever.
When young
We struggle,
Learn,
Are eager to succeed.
Time is not feared by the young.
Then it seems to stop –
Always.
Now time will not stop.
Now time will not delay.
It never stops –
Ever.